BEFORE YOU SELL YOUR HOME

How to: Stay Sane, Save Money, and Stay Legal

Maurine Dawson Grisso BSRE

ISBN: 1500677302
ISBN 13: 9781500677305

INTRODUCTION

Selling your home is one of the largest financial transactions you will make in your lifetime. It is very important to be prepared and have <u>all the information </u>before you make any decisions.

- Learn how to accurately price your home to keep the most money. The highest price is not always the best result – keeping the most money in your pocket at the end of the transaction is.
- Find what resources are available to you to get the help you might need.
- Get an overview of the whole transaction and become clear on what you hope to achieve when it's finished.
- Be aware of what paperwork is needed, including all necessary disclosures needed to sell in your state.
- Identify what you may need help with, and what you can do yourself to save the most money, when outlining the transaction.
- Know your options so that you can make the best choices. Whether you're going to sell your home yourself or find an agent to sell it for you, there is so much about selling your own home that can be a mystery.

BEFORE YOU SELL YOUR HOME

With this book, I will take some of the mystery out of the process.

My name is Maurine Dawson Grisso, and I understand that no two sales are ever the same. Starting with real estate in 1984, I bought a Help-U-Sell franchise. My phenomenal success in real estate is the result of 30 years' hard work, helping clients, and learning as much as I can about the market.

My office, Help-U-Sell of Santa Rosa, won the Pinnacle Office Award from 1996 to 2006, and in 2002, I became the Regional Director of Help-U-Sell for the Sacramento area. Eventually, I became the national trainer for Help-U-Sell.

With all my hard work, I would like to help you sell your home in the easiest and most manageable of ways. This is a process that can sometimes leave sellers feeling over-whelmed and unsure of their actions. The information and expertise in this guide will help you stay sane, save money, and stay legal.

DISCLAIMER

BEFORE YOU GET STARTED

These questions will help you decide whether you're ready for a home that's larger or in a more desirable location. If you answer yes to most of the questions in Group 1, it's a sign that you may be ready to move.

Questions - Group 1

1. **Have you built substantial equity in your current home?**
    Look at your annual mortgage statement or call your lender to find out. Usually, you don't build up much equity in the first few years of your mortgage, as monthly payments are mostly interest, but if you've owned your home for five or more years, you may have significant, unrealized gains.

2. **Has your income or financial situation improved?**
    If you're making more money, you may be able to afford higher mortgage payments and cover the costs of moving.

3. **Have you outgrown your neighborhood?**
    The neighborhood you pick for your first home might not be the same neighborhood you want to settle down in for

good. For example, you may have realized that you'd like to be closer to your job or live in a different school district.

4. **Are there reasons why you can't remodel or add on?**
   Sometimes you can create a bigger home by adding a new room or building up. But, if your property isn't large enough, your municipality will not allow it. Or if you're simply not interested in remodeling, moving to a bigger home may be your best option.

5. **Are you comfortable moving in the current housing market?**
   If your market is hot, your home may sell quickly and for top dollar, but the home you buy also will be more expensive. If your market is slow, finding a Buyer may take longer, but you'll have more selection and better pricing as you seek your new home.

6. **Are interest rates attractive?**
   A low rate not only helps you buy a larger home, but also makes it easier to find a buyer.

Questions - Group 2 - Special Circumstances

1. **Am I over my head in debt?**
2. **Do I need to start over?**
3. **Has there been a change in my lifestyle or financial status?**

If these questions in Group 2 fit you, go to the Special Circumstances in Chapter 6 for more information before moving on.

Ok, I have decided to sell my home. Now what?

Overview of the Process

- **Getting Your Home Ready to Sell**
- **Setting a Price for Your Home**
- **Marketing and Selling Your Home**
- **Working with a Buyer**
- **Paperwork, Realtors and More**
- **Special Circumstances**
- **Using a Broker?**

FORWARD

"I have been in the real estate business for over 30 years as an agent, broker of a large office, regional director for a national franchise as well as a C.O.O. for a national franchise. Maurine's guide on how to sell your home is the most comprehensive and easily understood outline I have read. Maurine covers all the bases from, staging the home for top dollar, to holding open houses, financing, inspections, and closing procedures and even covers special circumstances such as short sales. Tools provided in the appendix such as forms, disclosures and a glossary of terms are invaluable to anyone looking to sell their home. This is also a good reference book for new realtors, as well as a refresher for experienced realtors. I highly recommend this book for anyone interested in learning the home selling process."

John Powell
Help-U-Sell Galleria Realty
Designated Broker

"I've known Maurine for almost 35 years as a Real Estate Broker and Trainer. With this book she puts all her 30 years' experience into a guide that gives you step-by-step instructions and walks you through the entire process with check lists, forms and options. This book is a must read for anyone that has an interest in Real Estate."

Bob Robertson
G&R Services Inc.
President

TABLE OF CONTENTS

Chapter One:

GETTING READY!

Things to do before Putting Your Home on the Market

1. **Have a pre-sale home inspection**. Be proactive by arranging for a pre-sale home inspection. An inspector will be able to give you a good indication of the trouble areas that will stand out to potential buyers, and you'll be able to make repairs before open houses begin.
2. **Organize and clean**. Pare down clutter and pack up your least-used items, such as large blenders and other kitchen tools, out-of-season clothes, toys, and exercise equipment. Store items off-site or in boxes neatly arranged in the garage or basement. Clean the windows, carpets, walls, lighting fixtures, and baseboards to make the house shine.
3. **Get replacement estimates**. Do you have big-ticket items that are worn out or will need to be replaced soon, such as your roof or carpeting? Get estimates on how

much it would cost to replace them, even if you don't plan to do it yourself. The figures will help buyers determine if they can afford the home, and will be handy when negotiations begin.

4. **Find your warranties**. Gather up the warranties, guarantees, and user manuals for the furnace, washer and dryer, dishwasher, and any other items that will remain with the house.

5. **Spruce up the curb appeal**. Pretend you're a Buyer and stand outside of your home. As you approach the front door, what is your impression of the property? Do the lawn and bushes look neatly manicured? Is the address clearly visible? Are pretty flowers or plants framing the entrance? Is the walkway free from cracks and impediments?

OUTSIDE THE HOUSE

Curb appeal is one of the most important parts of showing your home because it's the first impression Buyers get of your home. If your home makes a good first impression, Buyers are more likely to come in and not be as critical. If they don't like the first impression, you run the risk of them not even coming in.

- First, if the **landscaping** is overgrown, trim it back so that Buyers can see the home. Add color with flowers.
- **Immediately fix anything** in the front of the house that is not working such as a gate that has a broken latch. If a Buyer's first impression is that something is broken, they will start to wonder what else you have let go.

- **Clean** windows and power wash the front of your house to make it look as clean as possible, and keep the front walk clean. Paint or refinish the front door if needed.

Case study

I had a Seller call me to sell his home for him in a stasis area with a good price on the home. So you would think that it would sell quickly.

His wife had a friend that was an agent so she wanted to sell the home through her. It was on the market for a long time and didn't sell. The husband asked me to come out, take a look at the property, and tell him why I thought it wouldn't sell. **It wasn't the price**... The front yard was dry and looked uncared for. The front gate latch was broken. The overall impression was gray and bleak.

I gave the Sellers some ideas of inexpensive fixes for the front of the home; they listed it with me at the same price. They did the fixes in one weekend, and the home looked loved and inviting when we were done.

We sold the home the next week at the full price.

INSIDE THE HOUSE

Sparkling Clean

Clean the windows and have the rugs cleaned. Use high-gloss furniture polish for all wood trim, cabinets and furniture. The Buyer has to be able to imagine their furniture in your home, so the more uncluttered you can make it, the better off you are.

De-clutter

The things that are very personal to you should be removed and stored away. Rent a storage unit if you have to. Box up some of the things that are cluttering your home and store them until you find your new home. Hold a garage sale to get rid of unwanted items and earn a little extra money too!

Light and Bright

- **In the living room** - Indirect lighting adds charm and elegance. Overhead lights can be harsh. Use pillows as accents to tie your furniture colors together. If you have a coffee table only, put one item on the table. Arrange the furniture in an open floor plan as much as possible.
- **In the bedrooms** - If you have lamps and indirect lighting, turn it on. Put a bed spread and pillows on the bed.
- **In the kitchen** - Buy small fluorescent lights and install under the cabinets to add light to the counters below the cabinets. Put fruit on the counter. Put all small appliances away out of sight; this will make the kitchen look larger.
- **In the Dining room** - Put a nice center piece or flowers on the table. Make sure all the chairs are pushed under the table.
- **In the bathroom** - Put guest soaps at the sink. Fold towels and put them on towel racks, and put a small bouquet of flowers on the counter. Put all toothbrushes, hair products, and shaving equipment out of sight. Use a small area rug if there's room for it. Keep shower curtains pulled back to the side.

... AND OF COURSE EVERYTHING SHOULD BE CLEAN AND SHINING!

To put the best face on a listing and appeal to Buyers who follow <u>Feng Shui principles</u>, keep these tips in mind.

1. **Pay special attention to the front door**, which is considered the "mouth of chi" (chi is the "life force" of all things) and one of the most powerful aspects of the entire property. Abundance, blessings, opportunities, and good fortune enter through the front door. It's also the first impression Buyers have of how well the Sellers have taken care of the rest of the property. Make sure the area around the front door is swept, free of cobwebs and clutter. Make sure all lighting is straight and properly hung. Better yet, light the path leading up to the front door to create an inviting atmosphere.

2. **Chi energy can be flushed away wherever there are drains** in the home. To keep the good forces of a home in, always keep the toilet seats down and close the doors to bathrooms.

3. **The master bed should be in a place of honor, power, and protection**, which is farthest from and facing toward the entryway of the room. It's even better if you can place the bed diagonally in the farthest corner. Paint the room in colors that promote serenity, relaxation and romance, such as soft tones of green, blue and lavender.

4. **The dining room symbolizes the energy and power of family togetherness**. Make sure the table is clear and uncluttered during showings. Use an attractive

tablecloth to enhance the look of the table while also softening sharp corners.

5. **The windows are considered to be the eyes of the home**. Getting the windows professionally cleaned will make the home sparkle and ensure that the view will be optimally displayed.

Source: "Sell Your Home Faster With Feng Shui", *by Holly Ziegler (Dragon Chi Publications, 2001)*

Holding a Successful Garage Sale

Garage sales can be a great way to get rid of clutter — and earn a little extra cash — before you sell your home. Follow these tips for a successful sale:

1. **Don't wait until the last minute**. You don't want to be scrambling to hold a garage sale the week before an open house. Depending on how long you've lived in the home and how much stuff you have to sell, planning a garage sale can demand a lot of time and energy.

2. **Get a permit if needed**. Most municipalities will require you to obtain a special permit or license in order to hold a garage sale. The permits are often free or very inexpensive, but still require you to register with the city.

3. **See if neighbors want to join in**. You can turn your garage sale into a block-wide event and lure more shoppers if you team up with neighbors. However, a permit may be necessary for each homeowner, even if it's a group event.

4. **Schedule the sale**. Sales on Saturdays and Sundays will generate the most traffic, especially if the weather cooperates. Start the sale early, 8 a.m. or 9 a.m. is best, and be prepared for early birds.

5. **Advertise**. Place an ad in free classified papers and Web sites, and in your local newspapers. Include the dates, time, and address. Let the public know if certain types of items will be sold, such as baby clothes, furniture, or weightlifting equipment. On the day of the sale, balloons and signs with prominent arrows will help to grab the attention of passersby.

6. **Price your goods**. Lay out everything that you plan to sell and attach prices with removable stickers. Remember, garage sales are supposed to be bargains, so try to be objective as you set prices. Assign simple prices to your goods: 50 cents, 3 for $1, $5, $10, etc.

7. **If it's really junk, don't sell it**. Decide what's worth selling and what's not. If it's really garbage, throw it away. Broken appliances, for example, should be tossed (know where a nearby electrical outlet is, in case a customer wants to make sure something works).

8. **Check for mistakes**. Make sure that items you want to keep don't accidentally end up in the garage sale pile.

9. **Create an organized display**. Lay out your items by category, and display them neatly so customers don't have to dig through boxes.

10. **Stock up on bags and newspapers**. People who buy many small items will appreciate a bag to carry their goods. Newspapers are handy for wrapping fragile items.

11. **Manage your money**. Make a trip to the bank to get ample change for your cashbox. Throughout the sale, keep

a close eye on your cash; never leave the cashbox unattended. It's smart to have one person who manages the money throughout the day, keeping a tally of what was purchased and for how much. Keep a calculator nearby.

12. **Prepare for your home sale**. Donate the remaining stuff or sell it to a resale shop. Now that all of your clutter is cleared out, it's time to focus on preparing your house for a successful sale!

SUMMARY

In short, look at your home as if you are the Buyer, and you are going to buy this house. Does it have enough curb appeal to get the Buyer inside the door, and once they are in, is it clean, uncluttered and bright with an open feeling? Can the Buyer picture their furniture in the rooms? Have you put away or stored items that stamp the home as yours?

I've sold my homes through Help-U-Sell twice now, and I would highly recommend them and their services to anyone. – Donald Gohranson

Help-U-Sell of Santa Rosa gave us wonderful, personalized support. They made sure we navigated this stormy market smoothly. The Help-U-Sell Smart Buyers program is a great deal. It helped us buy up to a better house in a better neighborhood. — Lori O'Hara & Michael Greenberg

They Made The Process Painless! Help-U-Sell of Santa Rosa helped me buy my home, even though I wasn't selling. They are very efficient and friendly people, and made me feel like I was their only client. Plus, they helped me save a ton! Help-U-Sell of Santa Rosa also set me up with a great lender who found me the best rate. – Bernie L

Chapter Two:

HOW DO I DETERMINE THE PRICE OF MY HOME?

When we talk about price, what we really mean is market value. The definition of market value is what a willing Buyer will pay for the home and what a willing Seller will sell the home for. Those two items together make up market value.

Market value is discovered by looking at the following:

1. What has sold in your immediate neighborhood in the last six months helps determine what your home will appraise for.
    *   Log on to Zillow.com and Trulia.com. These sites will give you an idea of your home's current value (*remember these prices are ballpark*).

2. What is for sale in your immediate neighborhood tells you about your competition.
  • Drive around the neighborhood and look for "For Sale" signs. Look in local papers for ads of homes for sale in your neighborhood.

3. Look at how many days those homes have been for sale. That will tell you if Buyers consider those homes to be a good value or if they are overpriced.

4. If your home has been on the market for more than 30 days without getting an offer of any kind, you should be prepared to at least consider lowering your asking price.

5. Consider the size of the home, the size of the lot, the age of the home, the condition of the home and the landscaping. Whether it's a 2-story or a 1-story home can make a difference.

Please note: What you paid for the home and/or how much money you have into the home really has no bearing on Market Value.

It's not uncommon for homes that are beautiful and well cared for to not sell and homes that require new paint, flooring and repairs to sell quickly. *The key is...*

Buyers buy what they consider to be a good value.

Tips for Pricing Your Home

- **Consider comparables.** What have other homes in your neighborhood sold for recently? How do they compare to yours in terms of size, upkeep and amenities?
- **Consider competition.** How many other houses are for sale in your area? Are you competing against new homes?
- **Consider your contingencies.** Do you have special concerns that would affect the price you'll receive? For example, do you want to be able to move in four months?
- **Get an appraisal.** For a few hundred dollars, a qualified appraiser can give you an estimate of your home's value. Be sure to ask for a market-value appraisal. To locate appraisers in your area, contact The Appraisal Institute or ask your REALTOR® for some recommendations.
- **Ask a lender.** Since most Buyers will need a mortgage, it's important that a home's sale price be in line with a Lender's estimate of its value.
- **Be accurate.** Studies show that homes priced more than 3 percent over the correct price take longer to sell.
- **Know what you'll take.** It's critical to know what price you'll accept before beginning a negotiation with a Buyer.

If you owe more than the value of the home (the mortgages), see Doing a Short Sale and Other Options in Chapter 6 - Special Circumstances.

SUMMARY

1. **Price it right.** Set a price at the lower end of your property's realistic price range.
2. **Prepare for visitors.** Get your house market-ready at least two weeks before you begin showing it.
3. **Be flexible about showings.** It's often disruptive to have a house ready to show at the spur of the moment. However, the more amenable you can be about letting people see your home, the sooner you'll find a Buyer.
4. **Anticipate the offers.** Decide in advance what price and terms you'll find acceptable.
5. **Don't refuse to drop the price.** If your home has been on the market for more than 30 days without an offer, you should be prepared to at least consider lowering your asking price.

HELP-U-SELL WAS GREAT! They helped us find the perfect place to spend the rest of our lives. Thank you Help-U-Sell, you were a blessing. – The Curriers

Thank You Help-U-Sell! Help-U-Sell sold our home in one week, and we saved $14,829! – Gary Stanley

I SAVED $13,550 & SOLD IN 24 DAYS! I sold my home with one open house and received more than my

asking price. Thank you Help-U-Sell for your profes-sionalism and quality service. – Robert Madrid

Is 12 hours to sell a house a new record? *I can't thank you enough for working with me on the sale of my home. Experience matters! From the moment of our first meeting you made the game plan of options very simple to navigate, and your refreshing and ex-tensive long term knowledge of the housing market and current trends made me very confident in my de-cision to enlist Help-U-Sell. It was obviously the right choice! 12 hours later I had a full price offer and saved more than $7,000 in fees! The service you provided and your attention to the details was just impeccable!*

Thank you again for your no nonsense and in-formed approach to real estate sales*. It has been such a pleasure to work with you, and I will highly recommend you to others. Great job Maurine!*

Respectfully
Cindy Taatjes

Chapter Three:

MARKETING YOUR HOME

Holding Open Houses

Check on the following items each time, as things pile up before showing your home:

De-clutter and clear off counters. Throw out stacks of newspapers and magazines and stow away most of your small decorative items. Put excess furniture in storage, and remove out-of-season clothing items that are cramping closet space. Don't forget to clean out the garage, too. You may want to hold a garage sale. (See tips for holding a garage sale)

Wash your windows and screens. This will help get more light into the interior of the home.

Make everything extra clean. A clean house will make a strong first impression and send a message to Buyers that the home has been well-cared for. Wash fingerprints from light switch plates, mop and wax floors, and clean the stove and refrigerator. Polish your doorknobs and address numbers. It's worth hiring a cleaning service if you can afford it.

Get rid of smells. Clean carpeting and drapes to eliminate cooking odors, smoke, and pet smells. Open the windows to air out the house. Potpourri or scented candles will help. Some agents tell their Sellers to bake cookies or bread just before people arrive so that the home smells like fresh baked goods.

Brighten your rooms. Put higher wattage bulbs in light fixtures to brighten up rooms and basements. Replace any burned-out bulbs in closets. Clean the walls, or better yet, brush on a fresh coat of neutral color paint.

Don't disregard minor repairs. Small problems such as sticky doors, torn screens, cracked caulking, or a dripping faucet may seem trivial, but they'll give Buyers the impression that the house isn't well maintained.

Tidy your yard. Cut the grass, rake the leaves, add new mulch, trim the bushes, edge the walkways, and clean the gutters. For added curb appeal, place a pot of bright flowers near the entryway.

Patch holes. Repair any holes in your driveway and reapply sealant, if applicable.

Add a touch of color in the living room. A colored afghan or throw pillow on the couch will jazz up a dull room. Buy new accent pillows for the sofa.

Buy a flowering plant and put it near a window you pass by frequently. Make centerpieces for your tables. Use brightly colored fruits or flowers.

Set the scene. Set the table with fancy dishes and candles, and create other vignettes throughout the home to help Buyers picture what it could be like to live there. For example, in the basement you might display a chess game in progress.

Replace heavy curtains with sheer curtains that let in more light. Show off the view if you have one.

Accentuate the fireplace. Lay fresh logs in the fireplace or put a basket of flowers there if it's not in use.

Make the bathrooms feel luxurious. Put away those old towels and toothbrushes. When Buyers enter your bathroom, they should feel pampered. Add a new shower curtain, new towels, and fancy guest soaps. Make sure your personal toiletry items are out of sight. Spruce up the bathroom for your guests with plush linens.

Send your pets to a neighbor or take them outside. If that's not possible, crate them or confine them to one room (ideally in the basement), and let the real estate practitioner know where the pets will be to eliminate surprises.

Lock up valuables, jewelry, and money. It's impossible to watch everyone all the time.

Hire a cleaning service. Buyers won't notice if your home is spotlessly clean, but they will notice if it isn't. A cleaning service tackles all those dusty places you might forget: baseboards, tops of picture frames, ceiling fans, etc.

Remove family photos. Yes, your children are stunning, and your animals are so cute! But Buyers need to see a neutral field where they can put down their roots.

Set the table. Stage your dining room table for a nice meal to encourage Buyers to imagine what it would be like to entertain in the house. Your best china and a new neutral tablecloth with matching napkins will help with the visualization.

Organize cabinets and drawers. Storage space is a vital selling point of any property. More is more when it comes to nooks and crannies, cabinets and closets. Cluttered linen closets, kitchen cabinets and bedroom closets make it appear that your home doesn't have enough storage. We guarantee that a Buyer is going to look.

Now the home is ready! When prospective Buyers come, have a guest book and ask people to sign in as they arrive. Try to stay with them and answer any questions they may have.

How can I have a successful Open House?
The good thing about using a broker/agent to help you sell your home is they have access to so many more Buyers than you do, because of all their other listings, that they can point

Buyers towards your home that might not otherwise see it. (See Chapter 7)

1. **Property signs** are important, as Buyers drive around areas where they want to live, looking for homes that might be for sale. Be sure you have a phone number on the sign so that they can contact you.

2. **Flyers** of your home are important. Have them at your home for Buyers to take away with them. Post them in your church and local supermarkets. Take a flyer around to all of your neighbors; invite them to an open house to see your home. Often, people want to live close to family or friends, so your neighbors may know of someone who would like to buy in your neighborhood.

3. **Network** with family, friends and coworkers. Tell your friends and all of your coworkers that your home is for sale, and give a flyer to anybody who will take one.

4. **Ads...Newspapers...Websites.** A large majority of Buyers these days look on websites to find homes for sale.

Check out these sites.

a.   www.zillow.com/homes/fsbo
b.   www.forsalebyowner.com
c.   www.owners.com
d.   www.homesforsalebyowner.com

Letting people know that your home is for sale includes websites, flyers, networking, and, very important, a sign in the yard.

I've had Sellers tell me that they don't want a sign in front of the house because they didn't want the neighbors to know that they were selling their home.

The pastor of my church was such a person. He didn't want the congregation to know he was leaving until he was ready for them to know. I told him about the importance of the sign. He agreed with me that if the house had not sold in two months I could then put up a sign.

Sure enough, two months later he told me to put up the sign. We had a full price offer in two days. A renter down the street had been looking for 6 months, and he only wanted to live in that neighborhood so his kids could stay in the same school. He didn't know that this home was for sale.

How do I write an ad that will help to attract Buyers?

BENEFIT HEADLINE

First, you need a benefit headline. A benefit headline is something that will attract the Buyer who would want your home. How would this home be a benefit to that Buyer?

For example, if you have a larger lot, a headline could be "Large Yard." This would attract a Buyer who has animals, who likes to barbecue, or be out in their backyard often. If the house has things that need to be done on it, you might want to say "Fixer - Needs TLC." If the house is in great shape, you might want to say for the headline "Move-In Ready." Here are a few other headlines in which the benefit will be obvious: "Horse Property"; "Seller Must Sell"; "Seller Transferred"; "Moving Out-of-State"; "Divorce"; "Can't Make Two Payments."

BODY OF THE AD

Talk about the home itself, the size of the home, and the size of the lot. Include the number of bedrooms, the number of bathrooms, if you have a family room, fireplace, or something really unusual about the home that you want to advertise such as a pool or spa.

Include the price of the home and how you can be contacted in the ad – maybe your phone number or your email address. As for the address of the home, you might want to state that it's in the northeast section if that is a very sought-after section of your city. Putting the address of the home in the ad is something that you must decide based upon whether you want them to drive by your home and look at the outside or if you want them to call you first for information.

Additional information about your home, which you may or may not want to put in your ad:

1. Walking distance to shops, parks, cafes, or cultural amenities

2. The feel, the floor plan, or the flow of the home

3. Storage space, privacy, or quiet outdoor living space

4. Granite, Corian, Maple, State of the art, Gourmet Wood floors throughout

5. Brand Names (Pottery Barn Chic), Calif Closets, Brand name appliances

6. Style of home or sought-after neighborhood

7. Built-in or custom desks, bookcases, closet organizers, garage storage systems, backyard composters, custom cabinetry, breakfast nooks, window seats

8. Solar panels, dual-paned windows

9. Kitchen luxuries, professional grade appliances, island, plentiful counter space, premium lot, extra bathrooms, mother-in-law unit

10. Prime neighborhood-price, prepaid HOA dues, closing costs credits

SAMPLE ADS

Move-In Ready!
A Stunning 2300 square foot, 4 Bedroom, 3 Bath home, located in beautiful Bennett Valley Heights with a gourmet Kitchen and tons of storage... $695,000. Call Owner for an appointment (707) 575-4444

Gardener's Delight!
3bds, 2ba on large lot - Family room with Fireplace $289,000. Open House May 2nd from 1 to 3pm. Call Owner (707) 575- 4444

Walk to Shops and Park!
Bright and sunny 2 bedrooms, 2 baths home with hardwood floors throughout, and a Large Master suite with Spa. 1500 square feet with fenced yard. $310,000. Call Owner (707) 575-4444

THANK YOU HELP-U-SELL! *We needed a quick sale and Help-U-Sell sold our house fast! Plus they saved us lots of money! Our family has referred several people to Help-U-Sell and will continue to do so as we know they will receive the same great service we did!* – The Mellados

I found a very nice investment property in Santa Rosa, all through Help-U-Sell. ***I had to close escrow in record time and they did it!*** *Thank you sincerely.* – Jesus Valencia

I SAVED $9,800!* Working with Help-U-Sell of Santa Rosa was a fantastic experience. I am so glad they were able to help me sell my house. – Linda Balcom

Chapter Four:

HOW DO I KNOW A BUYER IS QUALIFIED TO BUY MY HOME?

When a Buyer is interested, ask them the following questions:

1. **Have they applied for a loan**?

2. **Who is their Lender?** Ask to see a pre-approval letter. (If it's a cash offer, you need to see proof of the funds when they bring you the offer.)

3. **Do they have a pre-approval letter, not just a pre-qualifying letter?**

   - **Pre-qualify** means the Buyer has spoken to some-body, usually on the phone and based on what the

Buyer told them about their debt and income, the person on the phone said the Buyer should be qualified for a loan of a certain amount.

- **Pre-approval** means a Lender has taken a look at all the Buyer's debts, checked their credit report, and verified their income and down payment. Having looked at all this information, the Lender then says that the Buyer is pre-approved to buy a home for a certain amount.

You can take the Buyer more seriously when they have a pre-approval letter.

(See sample of pre-approval and pre-qualified letters in Appendix)

4. **Do they know what their credit report says?**
   Do they know what their FICO Score is? (See Glossary for explanation of FICO Score if you need more information)

5. **How soon do they want to buy?**
   If they are ready to buy now, get someone to help you with the offer such as an agent, lawyer or title company.

6. **Do they have an agent?** (Have the agent bring you an offer)

Help-U-Sell of Santa Rosa was there every step of the way in both transactions, handling all of the complicated *details of the escrow process. Plus I saved $12,275* on the sale of my home! I am very satisfied with Help-U-Sell of Santa Rosa.* – Dana Rodney

We saved $18,650* and we sold in 8 days! *The Help-U-Sell service was superb! We were very confident with the professional way they handled all the business. We would definitely use the Help-U-Sell service again.* – The Grimms

I listed my house on July 4th. *It sold on August 3rd, escrow closed on August 18th. The agents always have time to answer questions and explain details. They are well-trained, and the office is well-organized as a team. They very competently took care of all the details and everyone was always polite and helpful and very knowledgeable. I highly recommend this company!* – Barbara Shatto

Chapter Five:

I HAVE A BUYER, NOW WHAT?

Contracts

When you decide to sell your home yourself, you should obtain a copy of a Sales Contract that has fill-in blanks. You should not attempt to create or write any type of legal contract without professional assistance.

You can surf the web for the Department of Real Estate website in your state (it's a .gov website not a .com website). You can go to uslegalforms.com for basic forms, or surf the web for other suggestions. After we have a contract, what next?

Disclosure Forms You'll Need to Sell Your Home:

1. **Property disclosure form.** This form requires you to reveal all known defects to your property. Check with your state government to see if there is a special form required in your state.

2. **Purchasers access to premises agreement**. This agreement sets conditions for permitting the Buyer to enter your home for activities such as measuring for draperies before you move.

3. **Sales contract.** The agreement between you and the Buyer on terms and conditions of sale. Again, check with your state real estate department to see if there is a required form.

4. **Sales contract contingency clauses**. In addition to the contract, you may need to add one or more attachments to the contract to address special contingencies — such as the Buyer's need to sell a home before purchasing yours.

5. **Pre- and post-occupancy agreements**. Unless you're planning on moving out and the Buyer moving in on the day of closing, you'll need an agreement on the terms and costs of occupancy once the sale closes.

6. **Lead-based paint disclosure pamphlet**. If your home was built before 1978, you must provide the pamphlet to all Buyers. You must also have Buyers sign a statement indicating they received the pamphlet.

See Appendix for a complete list of disclosures needed for Sonoma County, Calif.
Go to a Title Company, a Lawyer, a Lender or the Internet to find a list of disclosures needed for your area.

What inspections do I need and when should I have them?

Most inspections on homes are negotiable between the Buyer and the Seller. The Buyer decides what inspections they want to have, and the Buyer and the Seller negotiate the cost of the inspections.

These inspections/tests/reports may include, but are not limited to:

1. Structural Pest Inspection
2. General Structural Inspection (Structural, Roof, Plumbing, Foundation, Heating & Cooling, Electrical, Windows, Etc.)
3. Pool/Spa Inspection
4. Fireplace/Chimney
5. Septic System Inspection (Environmental Health or Licensed Sanitarium)
6. Well (Well Portability, Reproductive Capacity, Mechanical Delivery System, Mineral Content)
7. Soil/Geological Inspections
8. Environmental Hazards Inspections Test (Radon Gas, Asbestos, Formaldehyde, Lead-Based Paint, Etc.)
9. Mold Inspection
10. Underground Tank
11. Public Search
12. Property Boundary Survey
13. Final Walk-Through (Pre-Close Escrow)

See Appendix for:

Checklist: 17 Service Providers You May Need When You Sell

Inspection Waiver From

Who pays for the repairs that may need to be done?

After the inspections are finished, the Buyer and the Seller may negotiate for the costs of repairs. In some cases the Lender may require certain repairs be completed before the title changes hands, e.g., a V.A. loan usually requires a Pest Report with a Section 1 clearance. Section 1 usually includes: termites, wood boring beetles, dry rot and fungus. These are things that when left unchecked can seriously damage and challenge the structure of the home. A Section 1 clearance states that this home is free and clear of all active infestation. But depending on how the contract is written, in most cases other repairs can be negotiated between the Buyer and the Seller.

How do I find out what disclosures are required in my state?

You can go to several different websites to find what is required in your state, such as the Department of Real Estate (your state).gov or uslegalforms.com.

See Appendix for:

A list of forms we use for California

Whether you are a Buyer or Seller, you want assurance that no funds or title of property will change hands until all instructions are followed and completed legally. With the increasing complexity of business law and tax structures, it takes a trained professional to supervise this transaction.

I've heard I need an escrow. Why do I need an escrow and what does an escrow do?

The escrow is a depository for all monies, escrow instructions, contract, and other documents necessary to complete the sale of your home. The escrow holder is a neutral third-party that acts for both the Buyer and the Seller. Escrow cannot be completed until the terms and conditions of all the instructions have been satisfied and all parties have signed escrow documents, based on the terms of the purchase agreement and the Lender's requirements. The escrow officer will prorate all of the taxes, the insurance costs, and all the other costs for the Buyer and the Seller. The following is an outline of an escrow officer's duties:

1. They receive signed purchase agreements and prepare escrow instructions.
2. Receive and deposit the Buyer's earnest money into the escrow account number.
3. Serve as a neutral agent and communication link for all parties in the transaction.
4. Order the preliminary title report.
5. Order pay off demands for any existing financing on your property.
6. Comply with the Buyer's Lender's requirements.
7. Make sure all contingencies and conditions have been met before close of escrow.

8. Prorate all taxes, interest, insurance, rents, and anything that might be due to the Buyer or the Seller as a result of this purchase.

9. Prepare all the documents needed for the completion of the transaction, including the transfer of the title to the property.

10. Arrange all the appointments for the Buyers and Sellers to sign the documents, as instructed. Request and receive funds from the Buyer and loan officers for the new loan on property.

11. Request issuance of the title insurance policies and the fire and liability property insurance.

12. Arrange for the recording of any deeds and documents as instructed.

13. Prepare final disposition of all funds in the escrow and prepare final accounting statements for all parties involved.

Why title insurance is important and why it is worth the money:

1. Title problems on properties are discovered in more than one third of residential real estate transactions. These defects must be resolved prior to closing. The most common problems are existing loans, unpaid mortgages, and recording errors of names, addresses or legal descriptions.

2. A homeowner's title insurance policy protects the owner for as long as he or she has an interest in the property, and the premium is paid only once at closing.

3. Title insurance is different from other forms of insurance because it ensures against events that have occurred before the policy is issued as opposed to ensuring against events in the future, as health, property or life insurance policies do. Title insurance is loss prevention insurance.

4. Also, when you go to sell the home, and you do not have title insurance on it presently, it creates what's called a cloud on the title; when the new Buyer tries to get title insurance, he or she will have a problem, and this can cost you a lot of money to rectify.

What is Agency?

Understand Agency Relationships

It's important to understand what legal responsibilities your real estate salesperson has to you and to other parties in the transaction. Ask what type of agency relationship your agent has with you:

- Seller's representative (also known as the listing agent or Seller's agent):
  - A Seller's agent is hired by and represents the Seller. All fiduciary duties are owed to the Seller. The agency relationship usually is created by a listing contract.

- Buyer's representative (also known as the Buyer's agent):
  - A Buyer's agent is hired by prospective Buyers to represent them in a real estate transaction. The Buyer's rep works in the Buyer's best interest

throughout the transaction and owes fiduciary duties to the Buyer. The Buyer can pay the licensee directly through a negotiated fee, or the Buyer's rep may be paid by the Seller or through a commission split with the Seller's agent.

Sub-agent

A sub-agent owes the same fiduciary duties to the agent's customer as the agent does. Sub agency usually arises when a cooperating sales associate from another brokerage, who is not the Buyer's agent, shows property to a Buyer. In such a case, the sub-agent works with the Buyer as a customer but owes fiduciary duties to the listing broker and the Seller. Although a sub-agent cannot assist the Buyer in any way that would be detrimental to the Seller, a Buyer-customer can expect to be treated honestly by the sub-agent. It is important that sub-agents fully explain their duties to Buyers.

Disclosed dual agent

Dual agency is a relationship in which the brokerage firm represents both the Buyer and the Seller in the same real estate transaction. Dual agency relationships do not carry with them all of the traditional fiduciary duties to clients. Instead, dual agents owe limited fiduciary duties. Because of the potential for conflicts of interest in a dual-agency relationship, it's vital that all parties give their informed consent. In many states, this consent must be in writing. Disclosed dual agency, in which both the Buyer and the Seller are told that the agent is representing both of them, is legal in most states.

Designated agent (also called appointed agent)

This is a brokerage practice that allows the managing broker to designate which licensees in the brokerage will act as an agent of the Seller and which will act as an agent of the Buyer. Designated agency avoids the problem of creating a dual-agency relationship for licensees at the brokerage. The designated agents give their clients full representation, with all of the attendant fiduciary duties. The broker still has the responsibility of supervising both groups of licensees.

Non-agency relationship (called, among other things, a transaction broker or facilitator)

Some states permit a real estate licensee to have a type of non-agency relationship with a consumer. These relationships vary considerably from state to state, both as to the duties owed to the consumer and the name used to describe them. Very generally, the duties owed to the consumer in a non-agency relationship are less than the complete, traditional fiduciary duties of an agency relationship.

We really liked how Help-U-Sell helped us! They were there when we needed them and found the house we needed. They were with us from beginning to end. We would definitely recommend Help-U-Sell to anyone trying to find a home. – The Olveras

We were very pleased with Help-U-Sell *and all of their staff, who were always available to answer my many questions, and we saved enough money to pay for our move. Thank you! – Frankie York*

Thank you! *I was 110% satisfied with my Help-U-Sell experience. They have all the industry know-how and were pleasing and professional to work with, and they saved me money with their reasonable and fair commission rates. I'm a convert. I'll never go back to the old ways of selling and buying. Help-U-Sell is the best! – David Schiltgen*

Chapter Six:

SPECIAL CIRCUMSTANCES

I owe more than what my home is worth, what are my options?

When you owe more money on your home than what it's worth or what you can sell it for, you have several options. You can short sell it, you can lease option it, you can do a contract of sale, or an all-inclusive deed of trust. When you start doing these more sophisticated transactions, I suggest you get help from a real estate broker or a real estate attorney. I think these deals are too complicated for you to do by yourself.

Short Sales: What to Do When the Sale Price Leaves You Short

If you're thinking of selling your home, and you expect that the total amount you owe on your mortgage will be greater than the selling price of your home, you may be facing a short sale. A short sale is one where the net proceeds from the sale won't cover your total mortgage obligation and closing costs, and you don't have other sources of money to cover the deficiency. A short sale is different from a foreclosure, which is when your Lender takes the title of your home through a lengthy legal process and then sells it.

1. **Consider loan modification first.** If you are thinking of selling your home because of financial difficulties and you anticipate a short sale, first contact your Lender to see if it has any programs to help you stay in your home. Your Lender may agree to modifications such as: refinancing your loan at a lower interest rate; providing a different payment plan to help you get caught up; or providing a forbearance period if your situation is temporary. When a loan modification still isn't enough to relieve your financial problems, a short sale could be your best option, if:

   • Your property is worth less than the total mortgage you owe on it.
   • You have a financial hardship, such as a job loss or major medical bills.
   • You have contacted your Lender and he/she is willing to entertain a short sale.

2. **Hire a qualified team.** The first step to a short sale is to hire a qualified real estate professional and a real estate attorney who specialize in short sales. Interview at least three candidates for each and look for prior short-sale experience. Short sales have proliferated only in the last

few years, so it may be hard to find practitioners who have closed a lot of short sales. You want to work with those who demonstrate a thorough working knowledge of the short-sale process and who won't try to take advantage of your situation or pressure you to do something that isn't in your best interest.

A qualified real estate professional can:

- Provide you with a comparative market analysis (CMA) or broker price opinion (BPO).
- Help you set an appropriate listing price for your home, market the home, and get it sold.
- Put special language in the MLS that indicates your home is a short sale and that Lender approval is needed (all MLS companies permit, and some now require, that the short-sale status be disclosed to potential Buyers).
- Ease the process of working with your Lender or Lenders.
- Negotiate the contract with the Buyers.
- Help you put together the short-sale package to send to your Lender (or Lenders, if you have more than one mortgage) for approval. You can't sell your home without your Lender and any other lien holders agreeing to the sale and releasing the lien so that the Buyer can get clear title.

3. **Begin gathering documentation before any offers come in**. Your Lender will give you a list of documents

required to consider a short sale. Typically, the short-sale "package" that accompanies any offer must include:

- A hardship letter detailing your financial situation and why you need the short sale
- A copy of the purchase contract and listing agreement
- Proof of your income and assets
- Copies of your federal income tax returns for the past two years

4. **Prepare Buyers for a lengthy waiting period.** Even if you're well-organized and have all the documents in place, be prepared for a long process. Waiting for your Lender's review of the short-sale package can take several weeks to months. Some experts say:

- If you have only one mortgage, the review can take about two months.
- With a first and second mortgage with the same Lender, the review can take about three months.
- With two or more mortgages with different Lenders, it can take four months or longer.

When the bank does respond, it can approve the short sale, make a counteroffer, or deny the short sale. The last two actions can further lengthen the process or put you back at square one. Your real estate attorney and real estate professional, with your authorization, can work with your Lender's loss mitigation department on your behalf to prepare the proper documentation and speed the process along.

5. **Don't expect a short sale to solve your financial problems.** Even if your Lender does approve the short sale, it may not be the end of all your financial woes. Here are some things to keep in mind:

- You may be asked by your Lender to sign a promissory note agreeing to pay back the amount of your loan not paid off by the short sale. If your financial hardship is permanent, and you can't pay back the balance, talk with your real estate attorney about your options.
- Any amount of your mortgage that is forgiven by your Lender is typically considered income, and you may have to pay taxes on that amount. Under the Mortgage Forgiveness Debt Relief Act and Debt Cancellation Act, a temporary measure passed in 2007, homeowners can exclude debt forgiveness on their federal tax returns from income for loans discharged in calendar years 2007 through 2012. Be sure to consult your real estate attorney and your accountant to see whether or not you qualify.
- Having a portion of your debt forgiven may have an adverse effect on your credit score. However, a short sale will impact your credit score less than foreclosure and bankruptcy.

Know your options!!

In our current economy, when speaking with home owners, their most common question is: "What are my options?"

So in answer to that question, I am compiling a list of different options for anyone who is concerned about their home payments, and what they could do if they lose their job or start to fall behind in their home payments. All of these options have an impact on your present life and on your future; some have more impact than others. Each option could have a significant impact on your credit rating.

Know your options before you make a move. In some cases you can try one option, and if that doesn't work for you, you can move on to another option.

Make A Choice. Look at the following options and the possible outcomes of that choice before you make any decision. You will feel much better if you make a choice, rather than just letting something happen to you.

"Choice is the key. You will feel much better if you make a choice rather than just letting something happen to you!"

Do Nothing. You can always do nothing – if you don't seek other options and you let nature take its course. This is sure to push you into foreclosure. The stress this puts on you and your relationships is far worse than any other option you might choose.

Pay off Mortgage. You can pay off the entire mortgage and solve all of these problems; however, this is not an option for most people.

Refinance. Refinancing your existing loan may help lower your payments depending on how much you owe on the property, how much the property is worth, and your current credit rating. Your best option is to check out rates with a reputable mortgage broker or banker.

Rent out the Property. Renting out the property may or may not be an option. If you are currently occupying your home, this may not be suitable. However, if this is a second home or an investment property, renting the property out could be viable.

Rental markets vary throughout the country, so it's a good idea to check with a reputable property manager and determine if the monthly rent will be acceptable to cover your costs or most of your costs.

Forbearance Plan. A forbearance plan will allow you to pay less than what you owe for your mortgage payment temporarily, and will sometimes let you postpone payments during a specific period of time. Typically the only way a Lender will consider this, is if you can show that you have a future lump sum of cash coming in that will bring you current or qualify you for a loan modification at the end of that forbearance period. This could be a payment such as a tax refund, an inheritance, or a bonus.

Loan Modification. Loan modification is an option many people are considering. This process includes a written agreement with your Lender that changes your loan agreement. Sometimes this can help make your payment more affordable by adding missed payments to your loan amount, changing an adjustable rate mortgage into a fixed rate, or even extending the number of years you can pay.

Loan modifications of the following sort are rare and often do not occur unless there are special circumstances. In some cases, a Lender may be willing to lower your interest rate which in turn will help make your payments more affordable. Another rare occasion in loan modification is that sometimes they will forgive a part of the principal debt. The instances that these two options occur are rare and unlikely to occur in most common cases.

Repayment Plan. If you are behind in your mortgage, talk with your bank. A repayment plan may be an option for you. A repayment plan will give you a fixed amount of time to repay the default amount. Usually this is done by combining part of what you owe with your regular payment. If you complete all the payments as agreed, you'll be completely current at the end of the repayment plan.

Traditional Sale. If you are one of the lucky homeowners that still contain equity in your property, this option is for you. Selling your home and paying off the mortgage with the proceeds is definitely an ideal option. It's an option many people do not have. This, however, could help alleviate any mortgage pressure you have.

Short Sale. A large majority of homeowners feeling mortgage pressure will be giving this option a good look. If your mortgage balance outweighs your home's price in the current market, the only way to sell the property is through a Short Sale. A Real Estate Broker, expert in short sales, finds a Buyer for your property at Market Value and negotiates with your Lender to accept less than what you owe on the property.

Deed in Lieu. With this option, you shall voluntarily transfer ownership of the property to your Lender to cancel your mortgage debt. There are usually some conditions with this option, and often they would require that you must have attempted to sell your home at fair market value for at least 90 days without success. However, these options usually are not valid if you have other liens or a second mortgage on the property.

Each Lender may have different requirements.

Bankruptcy. This does not save your home from foreclosure; it will postpone it for a short period of time. There are significant ramifications for any of these options. So, if you are considering bankruptcy, call an attorney who is an expert in bankruptcies.

NOTE: There are different types of bankruptcy.

Foreclosure. If you chose option number one above – "Do nothing" – you will usually arrive here sooner or later. Foreclosure happens when no agreement can be made with your bank, and you are in default on your mortgage with them. The bank will issue a "Notice of Default" and take back your home. Then the bank will sell it at fair market value according to the home's condition. You may have already been aware of some of these items, and understand what is needed or what kind of obstacles you may face; however, others may be unfamiliar with many of these items. Many individuals may not understand what these concepts "really" mean. If you want more information regarding these matters as they apply in California, please call me, Maurine Grisso at (707) 575-4444, and we will set up a consultation. Or contact me at www.maurinegrisso.com.

What are the tax ramifications of selling my home?

I suggest you go to a tax attorney to discuss tax ramifications of selling your home. A real estate broker is not licensed to give tax advice and should not do so. We are experts in selling and buying homes.

Thanks, Help-U-Sell!! *I sold a house using Help-U-Sell and I was so pleased by their advice and professional service, plus the savings in commission, that I used them again when I put another house on the market. They sold it the next day, and I saved five thousand-plus ($5000+) dollars!* – Scott Wilson

THEY HELD MY HAND ALL THE WAY THROUGH *Help-U-Sell was absolutely fabulous. They always answered my questions and concerns. I would not hesitate to recommend Help-U-Sell to anyone!* – Barbara Abrao

SHE DID THE JOB! *I been buying and selling Real Estate for over 25 years, and I have never met a more incredible Agent. Maurine has helped us from A to Z. She helped us get the home ready to show, price the home and plan the best marketing. We got a full price offer and we saved money by using her Set Fee concept. I am recommending her to my friends and family. – Madaline*

Chapter Seven:

IF I DO WANT OR FEEL I NEED HELP, HOW DO I PICK A REAL ESTATE BROKER?

It's not just about a real estate broker's credentials, or how long they've been in the business, or what their education is, or even how many homes they have sold.

Your Neighborhood
Do they understand the market in your area?

Marketing
Will they do marketing to find Buyers for your home?

Networking
Brokers and agents have access to other sources for Buyers that you don't have. The more Buyers you reach, the better chance you have for a good offer.

Communication

What's equally as important is, how well do they communicate with you?

Do they understand your needs and what you want to accomplish?

Do they understand your time constraints?
Do you feel that they listen to you, and are you comfortable with them? Do you feel that you both have a clear understanding of the situation? Do you both have a plan and a direction?

If your home falls in the special circumstances category, make sure your agent understands the ramifications of these circumstances and how to complete the sale.

There aren't any dumb questions, only unasked and unanswered questions.

Will this broker allow you to participate in the sale of your home to save money, and how much say can you have in the process?

I have been a Set Fee Broker for nearly 30 years. I own a Help-U-Sell office that charges a set fee to do all the functions that require a Real Estate License, and allows the Seller to do what they want to save money and still have the level of service they want. (Help-U-Sell has been operating since 1976. It is a national company)

The following are questions that have been asked about Set Fee Services:

How does Help-U-Sell work?

Help-U-Sell brokers and agents are fully licensed professionals, and they are members of their local Board of Realtors and of the National Association of Realtors. They work with both Buyers and Sellers, and provide a full range of real estate services. Help-U-Sell real estate differs from traditional brokers not in the scope of services provided, but in the dollar amount you pay for these services. Our brokerage charges a set fee for real estate services (as opposed to traditional 6% or 7% commission), which in turn helps you to retain a greater amount of equity, while still receiving all the real estate service you expect. Streamline business practices and a focus on marketing properties (rather than marketing ourselves) allow our brokers to spend their time working with Buyers and Sellers, as opposed to the traditional real estate brokers who spend the majority of their time managing offices and recruiting new agents.

How does fee for service work?

We believe that the traditional 6% commission is an outdated practice and has no correlation to the cost of performing a real estate transaction. Our goal is to provide a fair price for the cost of services rendered, much like any other professional service that consumers would pay for. Since the cost of doing business varies throughout the country, the set fee offered for our services also varies and is dependent upon the market – what doesn't change is the scope of services we provide. We perform all the same services as a traditional real estate company and often-times more services. Our unique marketing strategies drive an unprecedented amount of traffic to our website and offices, which results in many Buyers for our list-ings. Additionally, our streamline operations and cost ef-ficiencies translate into low overhead and savings that we pass along to consumers through our low set fee.

What are some of the advantages of using Help-U-Sell over another real estate company?

1. **Set Fee.** You know upfront exactly how much it's going to cost to sell your home and how much money you will retain.
2. **More Equity.** In most cases, our set fees are signifi-cantly lower than any other traditional real estate com-pany would charge for their commission; this means you retain more of your equity.
3. **More technology.** Help-U-Sell's proprietary technology allows you to obtain up-to-date information about your home sale quicker and more efficiently. In fact, with our technology you can be anywhere in the world and learn about the latest activity on your home.
4. **More experience.** According to the National Association of Realtors, the average agent typically handles less than 10 transactions a year, while our agents and bro-kers handle dozens, which means more in-depth market

knowledge, more experience solving problems and more value for our Buyers and Sellers.

WHO IS MY CUSTOMER?

My customer is someone who wants to save as much money as they can, have a stress-less transaction, be able to ask questions, and to be kept continually informed.

They want an agent who will listen to what they want, anticipates problems, gives them options, and explains the ramifications of the different options.

If you would like to contact me, my phone number is (707) 575-4444, my email is   mgrissohus@yahoo.com, and my website is maurinegrisso.com.

CONCLUSION

Real Estate has changed so much in the last 20 years. With the advent of the internet, Sellers and Buyers are more knowledgeable about Real Estate than ever. More information is available to the general public than ever.

At the same time, the legal side of selling and buying a home has also grown. The liability is greater, the amount of information available is overwhelming, and the paperwork is monumental. We jokingly say that an escrow can't close unless the file is at least 3 inches thick. Our E & O Insurance has also grown.

I choose to be a set fee broker because this is the way that I believe Real Estate is evolving. I see Real Estate sales falling into 3 basic categories:

1. The persons who just want it done now and don't want to be a part of the process. They don't care what they pay for services.

   (This is what Real Estate has been in the past for decades)

2. The persons who are willing to do part of the work themselves; who want to have someone else handle the legal part, the paperwork, and to assume that risk for a set fee.

    (This started with the advent of the internet)

3. The persons who want to do it all themselves and want to save as much money as possible.

    (These people are willing to put in the time, do the research, and take the risk of completing it all themselves)

I believe that a Seller can easily complete the part of the process that doesn't require a Real Estate license, and that they can (and should) pay themselves for that part of the sale.

The Real Estate Salesperson, on the other hand, is trained and skilled in the whole process. We have to take classes continually to maintain our licenses with the state to be able to sell Real Estate. We can take care of the rest of the process.

APPENDIX

Checklist: 17 Service Providers You May Need When You Sell

- Real estate attorney
- Appraiser
- Home inspector
- Mortgage loan officer
- Environmental specialist
- Lead paint inspector
- Radon inspector
- Tax adviser
- Sanitary systems expert
- Occupancy permit inspector
- Zoning inspector
- Survey company
- Flood plain inspector
- Termite inspector
- Title company
- Insurance consultant
- Moving company

Moving Checklist for Sellers

- Provide the post office with your forwarding address two to four weeks ahead of the move.
- Notify your credit card companies, magazine subscriptions, and bank of your change of address.
- Create a list of friends, relatives, and business colleagues who need to be notified about your move.
- Arrange to disconnect utilities and have them connected at your new home.
- Cancel the newspaper or change the address, so it will arrive at your new home.
- Check insurance coverage for the items you're moving. Usually movers only cover what they pack.
- Clean out appliances and prepare them for moving, if applicable.
- Note the weight of the goods you'll have moved since long-distance moves are usually billed according to weight. Watch for movers that use excessive padding to add weight.
- Check with your condo or co-op about any restrictions on using the elevator or particular exits for moving.
- Have an "open first" box with the things you'll need most, such as toilet paper, soap and paper towels, trash bags, scissors, hammer and nails, screwdriver, pencils and paper, cups and plates, water, snacks, and a toothbrush and toothpaste.

Plus, if you're moving out of town, be sure to:

- Get copies of medical and dental records and prescriptions for your family and your pets.

APPENDIX

- Get copies of children's school records for transfer.
- Ask friends for introductions to anyone they know in your new neighborhood.
- Consider special car needs for pets when traveling.
- Let a friend or relative know your route.
- Empty your safety deposit box.
- Put plants in boxes with holes for air circulation if you're moving in cold weather.

DISCLOSURES FOR THE STATE OF CALIFORNIA

FOR BUYERS:
*Agency
*Disclosure and Consent for Representation of More Than One Buyer or Seller
*Market Conditions Advisory
*Statewide Buyers and Sellers Advisory
*Sonoma County Disclosures and Disclaimers
*REO Advisory (if applicable)
*Short Sale Information and Advisory (if applicable)
*Verification of Property Condition

FOR SELLERS:
*Agency
*Disclosure and Consent for Representation of More Than One Buyer or Seller
*Carbon Monoxide Detector Notice
*Diseased Tree Disclosure
*Seller's Affidavit of Non-Foreign Status (FIRPTA)
*Home Owner Association Information Request (if applicable)

*Megan's Law Database Disclosure
*Lead-based Paint Hazards
*Market Conditions Advisory
*Mold Disclosure and Waiver
*Natural Hazards Disclosure Statement
*Pet and Animal Disclosures
*Statewide Buyers and Sellers Advisory
*Seller Property Questionnaire
*Short Sale Information and Advisory (if applicable)
*Supplemental Statutory and Contractual Disclosures
*Real Estate Transfer Disclosures Statements (TDS's)
*Water Heater and Smoke Detector Compliance
*Wood Stoves and Fireplace Inserts Advisory

INSPECTION/TEST WAIVER FORM

PROPERTY: _____

BUYER(s): _____

SELLER(s): _____

This waiver pertains to the Real Estate Contract dated:

Help-U-Sell of Santa Rosa highly recommends the buyer to order all inspections.

These inspections/tests/reports may include, but are not limited to:

1. Structural Pest Inspection   _____   _____

2. General Structural Inspection _____   _____
    (Structural, Roof, Plumbing, Foundation,
    Heating & Cooling, Electrical, Windows, Etc.)

3. Pool/Spa Inspection   _____   _____

4. Fireplace/Chimney   _____   _____

5. *Septic System Inspection*   _____   _____
    (Environmental Health or Licensed Sanitarium)

6. Well   _____   _____
   (Well Portability, Reproductive Capacity, Mechanical
   Delivery System, Mineral Content)

7. Soil / Geological Inspections   _____   _____

8. Environmental Hazards
   Inspections Test   _____   _____
   (Radon Gas, Asbestos, Formaldehyde,
   Lead-Based Paint, Etc.)

9. Mold Inspection   _____   _____

10. Underground Tank   _____   _____

11. Public Search   _____   _____

12. Property Boundary Survey   _____   _____

13. Other _____   _____   _____

14. Final Walk-Through   _____   _____
    (Pre-Close Escrow)

_____ has recommended the above inspections/tests/reports, to the Buyer(s). Buyer(s) have elected to waive those inspections/tests/reports where initials are present.

Upon waiving the opportunity to order any or all of these inspections/tests/reports,
Buyer(s) agree to release and forever hold harmless from any and all damages and/or loss the Buyer(s) may incur as a result of completing the purchase of the property without benefit of the recommended inspections/tests/reports.

_____ _____   _____ _____
Sales Associate   Date   Buyer   Date
(if applicable)

                              _____ _____
                               Buyer   Date

                              _____ _____
                               Seller   Date

                              _____ _____
                               Seller   Date

GLOSSARY OF REAL ESTATE TERMS

Addendum: Documents presented with an offer to purchase which clarify specific points of the contract as required by state law.

Adjustable-rate mortgage (ARM): A mortgage in which the interest rate increases or decreases over the life of the loan based on the fluctuations of a specified index rate (such as the six-month Treasury bill). This fluctuation usually results in a change of monthly payments. Most ARMs have rate caps which limit the fluctuation of your interest rate.

Amortization: The repayment of debt by means of installments of principal and interest (P & I) over a set period (term of the loan usually 30 or 15 years).

Annual percentage rate (APR): The entire cost of getting a loan, expressed as an annual percentage. Lenders are required by law to provide you with the APR calculation.

Appraisal: An appraisal is done by someone who is certified by the state to appraise property or someone who is a staff appraiser hired by the Lender. The final appraisal of your home will be ordered by the Buyer's Lender and paid for by the Buyer.

Buyer pre-qualification: Before a Buyer begins looking for a home, their Agent/Counselor or loan office gathers pertinent financial information from the Buyer to determine the price range of home the Buyer can afford.

Buyer pre-approval: A loan officer has obtained verification of the above financial information and has gotten a loan approval subject to an appraisal, a preliminary title report and a ratified purchase agreement for the home the Buyer has chosen.

Buydown: The ability to buy or obtain a lower-than-market rate from the Lender.

Closing costs: All costs, other than the loan origination fee, paid by the Seller or the Buyer when the loan is finalized.

Commitment: A promise by the Lender to make mortgage funds available for the purpose of financing a specific property. Such a promise is conditioned on Buyers having provided accurate qualifying information, as well as satisfying all underwriting requirements.

Conventional fixed rate mortgage: A mortgage in which the interest rate and payments remain constant over the life of the loan. It is not a government loan.

Counter Offer: If an offer to purchase comes in to a Seller which does not have desirable terms or price, the Seller can then make a counter offer. In some cases, the Buyer then makes another counter offer until a compromise can be reached.

Credit report: As part of the loan application process, the Lender requires a Buyer to pay for a credit report to get information on the Buyer's credit worthiness.

Deed of trust or mortgage: A deed of trust is a means of protecting a Lender's interest in a property. The deed is held by a trustee (third party) instead of by the Lender or the Buyer. In the case of a mortgage, the deed is held by the borrower.

Depreciation: Decrease in the value of property over a period of time due to use, wear, tear or obsolescence.

Disclosure statement: A detailed explanation of the specific features of the loan for which you are applying. It is required by law.

Discount: A reduction in the interest rate offered by the Lender, usually for an additional fee, referred to as discount points.

Earnest-money agreement: Also known as a sales contract, it is a written agreement between the Purchaser and Seller setting forth all terms and conditions of the sale. This good faith agreement is accompanied by a sum of money or equivalent (earnest money) given to bind the sale.

Equity: The interest or value which an owner has in real estate, over and above the mortgage or debt against it.

FHA Loan: A loan insured by the Federal Housing Administration and made by an approved Lender in accordance with FHA's regulations.

FICO Score: The FICO score is determined by a mathematical formula, and there is a direct correlation between your score and your ability to secure preferred loans or home mortgages.

FICO scores are based on several factors, with each given a certain amount of weight: Thirty-five percent of your credit score reflects payment history, including missed payments, late payments and number of accounts paid as agreed, according to MyFICO.com. The amount owed makes up 30 percent of your credit score, and 15 percent of your score relates to the length of your credit history (generally, the longer the better). FICO scores take new credit into account, affecting 10 percent of the score. Types of credit used account for another 10 percent, and, in general, long-term accounts, including student loans and home mortgages, have a more favorable impact on your credit score than revolving accounts, such as credit cards.

Mortgage insurance: Lenders require this when the borrower makes a low down payment, usually an amount less than 20 percent of the purchase price.

Land Contract (real state contract, contract for deed): A written agreement where the Seller retains the original mortgage and the Buyer does not get title to the property until the note is paid off.

Loan to value ratio: The relationship of the loan amount of the appraised value to the property or the sale price, which-ever is lower. The ratio is usually expressed as a percentage.

Lien: The right given by law to satisfy a debt. A legal claim of one person or company on the property of another for purposes of securing a debt.

Origination fee: Fee charged by the Lender to process a loan application and underwrite the loan.

Points: The amount equal to 1 percent of the principal amount of the loan. For example, if the loan is $ 50,000, a point would be $500. Points are charged by the Lender to increase the yield on a loan to make it comparable with other types of investments.

Rate lock-in: A guarantee that the interest rate will re-main the same for a specified period of time.

Second mortgage: A mortgage placed on a property which has second claim (or secondary rights of foreclosure) to a first mortgage on that property.

Secondary market: Investors who purchase loans from lending institutions, providing those institutions a second-ary source of funds (Fannie Mae, Freddie Mac, or Ginnie Mae).

Seller carry back: If a Buyer needs assistance with a down payment or closing costs, the Buyer may ask the Seller to carry a short-term percentage loan using a promissory note.

Set fee: A pre-determined fee paid by the Seller to the selling broker at closing for selling a property. (Some brokers charge a percentage commission rather than a set fee.)

Settlement: A process which is performed by a third party who holds earnest monies or valuable goods until the requirements of the Buyer, Seller, and Lender are satisfied. Earnest monies cannot be released until all parties agree to release the funds.

Title insurance: A policy which insures current ownership of the property regardless of previous claims against the property and insures the Lender's claim on the property resulting from the loan.

Underwriting: A series of criteria used by the Lender to determine whether a loan application should be approved or denied.

VA Loan: A mortgage loan on approved property made to a qualified veteran by an authorized Lender and guaranteed by the Department of Veteran Affairs in order to limit the Lender's possible loss.

ABOUT THE AUTHOR

Maurine D Grisso BSRE
Realtor-Broker/Owner

Affiliations:
National Association of Realtors
California Association of Realtors
Bay Area Real Estate Services MLS
Premier Agent for Trulia, Zillow, and Realtor.com

Professional Experience:
In 1984, she purchased her own Help-U-Sell office. Her phenomenal success in real estate is the result of 29 years of hard work.

Maurine was #1 nationwide in the Help-U-Sell System for 1998-1999 and she was in the President's Club for 6 years (1996 through 2001).

Help-U-Sell of Santa Rosa won the Pinnacle Award Office, 1996-2006.

In 2002, she became the Regional Director for Help-U-Sell for the Sacramento Area.

Her numerous achievements include being named Sacramento's 2004 Business Woman of the Year, and being honored by her colleagues at the Help-U-Sell Real Estate national convention with the prestigious Don Taylor Award.

Education:
Bachelor's degree in Real Estate
Trainer with Real Estate's premier training company, Floyd Wickman.
RDCPro Default School Graduate

Professional Associations:
- Five Star Institute Certified RES.NET Agent
- Frontline Real Estate Academy Certified Short Sale Specialist and Pre-Foreclosure Specialist
- Equator Platinum Certified Agent: REO Certified and Short Sale Certified
- Home Retention Consultant
- Professional DynaMetric Program certified PDP Administrator
- Affiliated with 5-Star Institute
- Open Door Institute
- LANCO Network
- REO Network since 2008

Personal Information:
Maurine, for over two decades, was a Motion Picture/ Television Actress, Motivational Speaker, College Educator and Curriculum Writer. Her written article on "Helping Seniors Sell Their Homes," which was a look at assisting seniors whose time has come to sell their all too familiar homestead, has been picked up by senior publications nationwide. She was also the Real Estate expert on "Ask the Experts" for KFTY TV. In

addition to her tireless enthusiasm for Real Estate, Maurine is also a strong supporter of community causes. She has been on the Board of Directors for the Easter Seals Society and was a sergeant of arms for the Santa Rosa East Rotary Club for 5 years.

CLIENT EXPERIENCE

See three following examples of how I work with clients:

Example 1

Need: Wanted to relocate from California to Florida

Goal: Get enough money out of the sale of her present home to pay off mortgages and to buy a place in Florida that would be free and clear of all mortgages. Because this money that she was getting out of this home was her retirement money, it was very important to do everything she could to maximize the value of this present home.

Solution: List the upgrades and improvements that could be done with very little money and relatively quickly. Have a plan to stage the home, price it aggressively and plan the marketing of the home, including marketing it on as many websites as possible, contacting possible Buyers and networking with other agents.

Execution: We went from room to room; the Seller decided what she could do to de-clutter and to clean up the house to make it as clean and spacious as possible, to polish all wooden surfaces with a high-gloss furniture polish. Clean the windows inside and out. Power-wash the front and back of the house cut the grass and do a little inexpensive landscaping.

Results: The Seller said, "I been buying and selling Real Estate for over 25 years, and I have never met a more incredible agent. Maurine has helped us from A to Z. She helped us get the home ready to show, price the home and plan the best marketing. We got a full price offer and we saved money by using her Set Fee concept. I am recommending her to my friends and family."

Example 2

Need: Seller lost his job and could no longer afford to keep up the payments on his home. He had gone through all of his savings and his retirement trying to maintain the home payments. He could not do a regular sale on his home because he owed more money on the home than what it was worth.

Goal: Get out from under the heavy payments and all of the other money problems this was creating for him and for his family and to start over again.

Solution: Do a Short Sale on the home. Get help with planning to pay off all of the credit card debts and get into a new place to live.

Execution: We marketed the home and found a Buyer. We helped the homeowner put together a short sale package for the Lender. The short sale package explained their hardship, contained the contract from the Buyer, the comparables which justify the price we sold it for, the estimated closing statement and requests that the Lenders take less money than what is owed on the home and forgive the rest of the debt. We followed through every week with the Lender on the short sale until it was completed; it took about two months for all the paperwork to be reviewed by the Lender. The Seller found another job and was able to make enough money to move into a smaller place and start his life over again.

Results: We had 4 offers on the home, got it into escrow in 3 days and completed the sale in record time.

Example 3

Need: The homeowner had passed away, and the home was inherited by survivors. The home needed to be sold and the inheritance distributed among the heirs. The home was a large parcel of land that could be used as a horse ranch.

Goal: Find out what the heirs expected to get from the sale of the home. Obtain an appraisal so all heirs will have realistic expectations. Get the home ready to sell.

Solution: Price the home. Market and network the home through websites and in places where horse people frequent.

Execution: Send flyers to Buyers in database that wanted horse property. Post flyers in Saddle and Feed stores. Keep heirs updated weekly. Put property listing into MLS. Do a Brokers' Open House.

Results: We found a Buyer that wanted a property they could keep horses in. We put the home into escrow and closed the sale in 32 days.